# Life's changing scenes

### A weekly reader

———— // ✳ // ————

To

..........................................................................

From

..........................................................................

*Jarrold Colour Publications, Norwich.*

The pinnacled tower of Great Malvern Priory, Worcestershire, dominates this
wintry scene

## Acknowledgements

The scripture quotations contained herein are from the Revised Standard Version Bible, © 1946, 1952, 1971 by the Division of Christian Education of the National Council of the Churches of Christ in the USA, and are used by permission.

# *New Year*

A new year means the possibility of new beginnings. That can seem daunting, even frightening. All kinds of new experiences may lie ahead of us. How do we know we shall be able to cope with them? Maybe if things went wrong last year we fear we shall just get into the same muddle this time round.

Look at it another way. Each new year at school I was given new, clean exercise books. The old tatty, blotted ones with all the red ink on them were thrown away, or, at least, put on the shelf. The new, fresh books gave me the chance to try again. A new year gives us new opportunities, new possibilities, the chance to start again. And we need not step out into it on our own.

> *Be strong and of good courage; be not frightened, neither be dismayed; for the Lord your God is with you wherever you go.*
>
> Joshua 1:9

Frost traces delicate patterns on fallen oak leaves

# Winter Storms

*O God, our help in ages past,*
*Our hope for years to come,*
*Our shelter from the stormy blast,*
*And our eternal home.*

Isaac Watts

Winter can bring wild weather when we are glad to stay safe at home. On a dark winter's night it's good to draw the curtains tight and warm ourselves by the fireside, sheltering from the 'stormy blast'.

Those words from the hymn often sung on Remembrance Sunday speak of stormy experiences in our lives. Those times when we seem to be lashed and blown about by hard things happening to us. When we are in the centre of the storm it is important to remember that we have come through hard times in the past and to hang onto the hope of a better future. And when we seem to be losing our foothold we can remember that 'shelter' we are offered 'from the stormy blast'. The refuge which can be our home for ever.

Deep snow at Ashwellthorpe, Norfolk

Snow scene at Barton Seagrave, Northamptonshire

# *Winter Beauty*

There can be great beauty in a winter landscape. The strong outline of a mighty oak tree standing starkly against a February sky. The delicate embroidery of hoarfrost on windows, branches and even cobwebs. The cleanness of new snow falling gently, silently. The magic of waking to a shining, white world. The sun sliding down behind a dark hill like an orange ball. The sparkle of stars in a velvet sky. The faint blue light of the moon shining on a frosty garden.

> *Praise the Lord!. . . Praise him, sun and moon,*
> *praise him, all you shining stars! Praise the Lord*
> *from the earth. . . snow and frost, stormy wind*
> *fulfilling his command!. . . Praise the Lord!*
>
> Psalm 148:1,3,7,8,14

Cley Mill, Norfolk on a crisp winter's day

# *Thank you*

I was in bed with flu and feeling wretched. The worst of the aches and pains had gone but I felt weak and wobbly. Reading made my eyes hurt and the radio gave me a headache. To make matters worse I was having to miss a whole round of interesting activities. Life seemed pretty grey. Then Anne called to see me. Calm, gentle, humorous and friendly, she had brought me a pot of flowering plants. Deep pink, yellow and blue with bright green curly leaves, the little plants cheered me up. For the first time that day I noticed that a thin winter sun was shining through my window. I planned where I would put the plants in the garden when they had finished flowering. Already I was feeling much better! Thank you, Anne.

*Be kind to one another*
Ephesians 4:32

The cheering sight of spring flowers. . .

. . .can brighten the dullest day

'He made their glowing colours. . .'

# He Made Them All

*All things bright and beautiful,*
*All creatures great and small,*
*All things wise and wonderful,*
*The Lord God made them all.*

*Each little flower that opens,*
*Each little bird that sings,*
*He made their glowing colours,*
*He made their tiny wings.*

Is this the most loved of all children's hymns? It was written more than a hundred years ago by a young Sunday School teacher, Fanny Humphreys who became Mrs C.F. Alexander. She wrote it to help children understand that the world they saw around them, beautiful, intricate, infinitely varied was made by God, Creator of Heaven and Earth.

Words written for little children, but they still speak to us if we will open our eyes and look.

'. . .he made their tiny wings'

# Joy in the Morning

'Heralds of Spring' they are rather grandly called. The little flowers that come through the cold ground in early Spring. Aconites and snowdrops, crocuses and miniature iris and, maybe against a wall or fence, a great bush of yellow winter jasmine, all defying the bitter weather. Later there will be hyacinths and daffodils and then bluebells in the woods. The bulbs were buried underground through the dark winter months. Maybe we had forgotten they were there. Now they surprise us with their colour and beauty. They can remind us that hope can sprout again after a time of darkness; that peace can blossom again after a storm; that from the deepest sadness joy can grow again.

*Weeping may tarry for the night, but joy comes with the morning.*

Psalm 30:5

'Heralds of Spring' – aconites. . .

. . .and bluebells

'A haze of bluebells. . .'

# Clear Skies

A day in Spring. Clear sky after grey clouds, warm sun after chill rain. Everywhere, in the woods, in the fields, in the garden there are things to delight the senses. A haze of bluebells, the blackbird's song, the softness of pussy willow, the scent of primroses. There is new growth wherever you look. The colours are fresh and bright, the scents delicate and haunting. Is this the day to put work aside for a while so you can stand and stare or take a walk? Just to enjoy – and be thankful?

*Lo, the winter is past, the rain is over and gone.*
*The flowers appear on the earth,*
*The time of singing has come,*
*And the voice of the turtledove is heard in*
*   our land.*
*The fig tree puts forth its figs and the vines are*
*   in blossom;*
*They give forth fragrance.*

Song of Solomon 2:11-13

'. . .new growth wherever you look.'

## He First Loved

A group were talking about belief in God. They agreed that many people can say they believe in God, but find it difficult to talk about loving him. You can't make yourself love out of a sense of duty. Where does love come from?

Then one told a story about the time when her first baby was born. For many months she had felt guilty because she did not feel the great warmth of love for her baby she had expected. She looked after her carefully, but without joy. Then, one day, the baby was sitting across the room on the knee of a friend. Catching sight of her mother, the baby's face broke into a great, beaming smile. Suddenly the mother realised that her baby loved her! Knowing that, allowing herself to enjoy being loved, was all it took for love to begin to grow in return.

*We love, because he first loved us.*
1 John 4:19

Out for a stroll at Hellidon, Northamptonshire

Springtime beauty at Letcombe Bassett, Oxfordshire

# Just As I Am

Charlotte Elliott was a Victorian lady who led a long and rather uneventful life. When she was 32 she had an illness which left her an invalid. One day a travelling preacher visited her home. At the time she was feeling depressed and useless. She wanted to find peace through faith in Jesus Christ but told the preacher,

'I do want to come to Christ but I don't know how.'

'Come to him just as you are.'

Twelve years later she was living with her brother. One day she had to stay at home because she was not feeling well enough to go out with the rest of the family. The old feelings of depression and uselessness came over her again. Then she remembered the preacher's words and began to write a hymn.

Charlotte Elliott wrote her hymn for her own comfort. It has brought help and comfort to countless thousands down the years.

*Just as I am, without one plea*
*But that thy blood was shed for me,*
*And that thou bidst me come to thee,*
*O Lamb of God, I come.*

*Just as I am, though tossed about*
*With many a conflict, many a doubt,*
*Fightings and fears within, without,*
*O Lamb of God, I come.*

# *Gardening*

Gardening is a pleasant hobby for some people – and a burden to others. The joy of a garden is that it is ever changing, particularly during the early summer months. Each day you can enjoy new growth and development. The trouble with gardening is that it takes hard work to achieve the lovely effects. Armchair gardeners may dream their dreams but unless the spade is lifted the weeds take over. The effort can be backbreaking – but the rewards heartening.

Gardening requires patience, because seeds and little plants take time to grow. But the patience is worthwhile when the dreams become reality. Sometimes you have to accept disappointment when things just do not grow as you had hoped. But then there will be times when you are delighted by better results than you had looked for. Perhaps it is not surprising that some find that gardening brings them closer to the great Creator.

*The Lord God planted a garden in Eden, in the East; and there he put the man whom he had formed. . . to till it and keep it.*

Genesis 2:8,15

This charming cottage is in Chalfont St Giles, Buckinghamshire

Trafalgar Square, London

# *You are Mine*

A crowd can be a very lonely place. Everybody else seems to be rushing along and no one knows us. Sometimes we are made to feel just a number on a list, or an object on a conveyor belt. Yet each of us is different and we all have qualities and talents that are unique. We think it is wrong to be conceited, but isn't it also wrong to undervalue ourselves? Rather we should find out what we are good at and develop that gift. A talent can be for some great creative work or it can be for something homely and simple. Whether it is making glorious music or a good cup of tea or arranging flowers, we all have gifts to share. That way we shall find friends – and find ourselves.

*I have called you by name, you are mine.*

Isaiah 43:1

Enjoying the sunshine in Parade Gardens, Bath

# The Peace of God

Times when we can be on our own are very important. They can be oases of peace which refresh us and build us up to cope with the duties and responsibilities of life. Times on our own can be specially valuable if we seek out peaceful places, peaceful occupations, peaceful things to look at, peaceful things to think about. Some moments spent in a quiet church, a walk in the country, knitting by the fireside, listening to music, enjoying a painting, reading a good book, just stroking the cat. We need to make peaceful spaces in our lives.

> *The peace of God, which passes all understanding, will keep your hearts and minds in Christ Jesus.*
>
> Philippians 4:7

'oases of peace' – at Southport Botanic Gardens, Lancashire...

. . .and at Stanway, Gloucestershire

A glorious burst of colour – delphiniums in full bloom

# Free Gifts

'Send for your free gift' say the advertisers, trying to entice us into spending our money. Go outside on a warm summer's day and you will find free gifts all around you. From magnificent garden displays to humble wild flowers, the colour and scent are there for your pleasure. Feel the warmth of the sun, the gentle breeze, enjoy the soft grass to sit on. Take nothing for granted but accept it all gratefully. And, if you will, see the hand of the Creator in it all.

*God saw everything that he had made, and behold, it was very good.*

Genesis 1:31

The delicate blossoms of the flowering currant

# Rainy Day

A rainy day can be a disappointment if plans have to be set aside or an outing cancelled. But there is beauty in rain as it softly falls and the scent of a summer garden after a shower, and the sparkle of wet blades of grass can make any inconvenience worthwhile. In any case, we need rain for growth and it would be foolish to resent it. Better by far to appreciate sunshine and showers as part of the natural cycle of things, and try to say thank you.

> *Sing to the Lord with thanksgiving; . . .*
> *he covers the heavens with clouds,*
> *he prepares rain for the earth,*
> *he makes grass grow upon the hills.*

Psalm 147:7,8

A stunning rainbow at Craignure on the Island of Mull

An overcast sky forms a dramatic backdrop for Stornoway Harbour, Lewis

A popular holiday spot – sheltered Towan Beach at Newquay, Cornwall

# Holidays

The thought of a Summer holiday can cheer up the greyest day. Whether it is a fortnight in the sun or a few day outings, we need to 'get away from it all' for a little. Even if we enjoy the everyday routine of life, a change is important. It gives us vital rest and refreshment. It can give us a time to look at our lives and see where we are going. A holiday can give us new perspectives, new ways of looking at life. We can make new friends, develop new interests and bring home a host of memories to refresh us as we pick up that routine again.

*He makes me lie down in green pastures,*
*he leads me by still waters; he restores my soul.*

Psalm 23:2

Boats wait at Lyme Regis, Dorset

# Seaside

Crashing waves against a cliff, the tang of salty air, strong, fresh wind, birds wheeling in the sky. Or the endless, gentle rhythm of waves on a sea shore when the sun shines on sparkling water and golden sand. Or the happy sound of people enjoying a sea bathe. Or the excitement of being in a boat and watching as a path seems to be cut through the water. Or the inspiration of a walk on the shore at the end of the day, when the water is calm and still, the beach empty and silent and the setting sun turns the sea into a carpet of liquid red and gold and at last to silver in the moonlight.

*The sea is his, for he made it.*

Psalm 95:5

Old holiday traditions still give pleasure

Sun-worshipping at St Ives, Cornwall

# Postcards

'Wish you were here' say the traditional holiday postcards. We send postcards as a greeting to our friends and are glad to receive them in return. Like the snapshots we take and stick into albums when we get home, they are reminders of special days. Days when we went to new places or revisited old haunts. They are like the pictures we all carry in our minds, memories we treasure of people, places and events which we can bring out from time to time to relive good times. Especially when life seems hard and things are not going well with us, reminders of happy days can give us the courage to carry on.

*O give thanks to the Lord, for he is good, for his steadfast love endures for ever.*

Psalm 136:1

Bradwell, Derbyshire – in the heart of the Peak District

# *Home*

When we have been away for a while there can be something comforting in the words 'let's go home'. It is good to get away, but good to get back. Home, after all, is our place, the place where we can be most ourselves, surrounded by friendly, familiar faces and objects. And if home is emptier than it once was, we have our memories to enjoy. Sometimes the ordinariness of our day to day lives seems monotonous, even boring. It is only when we come back home after a break that we realise home is the best place for us to be.

*May the Lord deal kindly with you. . .
the Lord grant that you may find a home,*
Ruth 1:8,9

Traditional thatched cottage at Billington, Bedfordshire

'All is safely gathered in' – St Mary's Church, Dedham, Essex

# *Harvest Festival*

It is a tradition at Harvest time to have a Festival in churches. People bring offerings from fields and gardens and hedgerows, filling the church with the colour and scent of late Summer. Probably somewhere there will be a Harvest loaf, perhaps made in the shape of a sheaf of corn.

Bread is good to make, but it takes time. Time for the yeast to bubble and grow and time for the dough to rise. But it is worth waiting for, there is nothing like the smell of a new baked loaf.

Truth to tell, the flowers and vegetables of the Harvest festival display have also taken time to come to fruition. And now, at the season we call the 'Crown of the Year' we can say that, like all good things, they were worth waiting for.

> *The earth has yielded its increase; God, our God has blessed us.*

Psalm 67:6

Beech nuts – eagerly sought by woodland creatures such as squirrels, dormice and deer

# Abide With Me

*Abide with me, fast falls the eventide;*
*The darkness deepens, Lord, with me abide!*
*When other helpers fail, and comforts flee,*
*Help of the helpless, O abide with me.*

When Henry Lyte wrote 'Abide with me' he knew his life was coming to an end. More than that he was facing a time of deep personal sadness. He had been vicar of the Devon fishing village of Brixham for more than twenty years and now he felt he was being deserted by some of the leaders of his church. He turned in faith and trust to the place where true help is to be found. The hymn was his parting gift to his parish. He could not have guessed how many people it would help in the years to come.

*Hold thou thy Cross before my closing eyes;*
*Shine through the gloom, and point me to*
*the skies;*
*Heaven's morning breaks, and earth's vain*
*shadows flee;*
*In life, in death, O Lord, abide with me!*

'. . .fast falls the eventide' – at Loch Insh near Aviemore, Highland

Autumn beauty – at Aber Glaslyn, Gwynedd. . .

# *Autumn Leaves*

In the Autumn garden the leaves pile up, drifts of yellow and brown, green and gold. If left, they will look good for a while and then rot into a soggy, dark mass. Best to rake them up and leave the grass and flower beds clear of suffocating debris.

So in our lives, we need to clear away the debris which is holding us back from growth. Some of it served a purpose once but is no use any longer – ideas or attitudes which we have grown out of. Some of it is just rubbish we should have cleared out long ago – old habits, the memories of things we did wrong. Raking it all away will free us to live healthier lives and, like the plants in the garden, put out new growth.

> *Create in me a new heart, O God, and put a*
> *new and right spirit within me.*
>
> Psalm 51:10

. . .and in a Norfolk glade

# Patience

Planting a bowl of bulbs is a hopeful thing to do. It requires patience, because it will be several weeks before the green shoots show. It depends on a certain trust that the dry, brown, dead-looking bulb will one day produce a lovely flower. Patience is rewarded and trust confirmed when a room is filled with fragrances. Sometimes the best things have to be waited for and we must accept that there will be no quick results or instant effects. Sometimes we have to do things in trust, believing that there will be a good outcome eventually. The waiting and trusting can be hard but the fulfilment is glorious.

*Be still before the Lord and wait patiently for him.*

Psalm 37:7

The lovely blooms of hyacinths

Waiting for the spring

Night scenes – at Westminster, London. . .

# The Dark

As the nights draw in we become more conscious of the dark. The friendly lights of home are a welcome sight, representing as they do warmth, familiarity and security. Some people remain afraid of the dark all their lives, though they may not care to admit it. For others, the dark can seem to echo a bleakness in their own hearts. When we dread the dark, whether it is outside the door or that deeper darkness within ourselves, we can look for comfort to the one who called himself *The Light of the World.*

> *In him was life and the life was the light of men. The light shines in the darkness, and the darkness has not overcome it.*

John 1:4,5

. . .and the River Tyne and Tyne Bridge, Tyne & Wear

# The Oak Tree

Around the foot of the great oak tree the ground is littered with acorns and their little pipe-like cups. The tree has stood for many years, growing to maturity through the rolling cycles of the seasons. It began life as one of the little brown acorns, so insignificant that no-one bothered to pick it up. But the acorn had new life locked inside its shell, and roots and shoots broke through. We need not despise any fresh start or new beginning because it seems small or insignificant. If it has life within it, and the right soil, it will grow. Look what happens to some acorns!

*Out of the ground the Lord God made to grow*
*every tree that is pleasant to the sight and good*
*for food.*

Genesis 2:9

Oak leaf and acorns

Grazing in the New Forest

Stepping stones at Gargrave, Yorkshire

# Remember, Remember

November is a good month for remembering how important it is to be remembered. It is terrible to think you have been forgotten. What a joy when someone remembers you. *'You won't remember me . . .' 'Oh but I do . . .'* The card or phone call or visit on an anniversary, happy or sad, can mean so much. It is a way of saying, *'I value you'*. And when times are hard and the blues have hit us and we think everyone has forgotten us, it is important to remember that our Heavenly Father never forgets us.

> *Jesus said 'Are not five sparrows sold for two pennies? And not one of them is forgotten before God . . . Fear not; you are of more value than many sparrows.*

Luke 12:6,7

Golden reflections on Derwentwater, Cumbria

# *Windy Day*

It has been windy all day, a great, strong wind, hard to battle against as you try to make your way outdoors. The trees are being tossed violently about, their branches creaking under the strain as the wind forces against them. The last, lingering leaves are torn off and blow around in a frenzied dance. The trees survive the force of the wind because their roots grow deep. So they are battered by the onslaught but they do not fall.

> *Jesus said 'Everyone who hears these words of mine and does them will be like a wise man who built his house upon the rock; and the rain fell, and the floods came, and the winds blew and beat upon that house, but it did not fall, because it had been founded on the rock.'*
>
> Matthew 7:24-25

The wild and haunting beauty of Duart Castle on the Island of Mull

'battered by the onslaught'

A winter-coated woodland

# New Life

The garden looks dead at this time of year. The plants are cut down and some, blackened by the frost, are pulled up and thrown away. The trees and many shrubs are bare. Even the winter jasmine has no flowers. Yet here and there, if you look carefully, it is possible to see signs of growth. There are green buds on the jasmine which will flower in the warmth of the house, and the first tips of daffodils are beginning to show through the ground.

Where there seemed to be death, there is new life.

> *He who sat upon the throne said 'Behold,*
> *I make all things new.' Also he said, 'Write this,*
> *for these words are trustworthy and true'.*

Revelation 21:5

The pretty flowers of jasmine, yet to come

# The Star

A clear December night, with a sharp frost making the ground sparkle in the moonlight. The dark velvet sky is bright with stars. Indoors, maybe you are beginning to sort out the Christmas decorations and plan presents and feasts. Tinsel and turkey can be offerings of love to our families. As we write cards and wrap presents we can say a prayer and send that too. The stars in the sky are a sign to us, a reminder of the star that shone over a stable at Bethlehem. As we prepare our homes so we can prepare our hearts for the coming of Christmas.

*We have seen his star in the East and are come to worship him.*

Matthew 2:2

The water ripples gently on Loch Duich, Highland

St Mary's Church, Beverley, Humberside

Christmas lights on the Promenade, Cheltenham, Gloucestershire

# Candles

Now that our homes are lit by electricity we only use candles as decorations. Particularly at Christmas time we light them in honour of the Light of the World. In some places there is a tradition of placing lighted candles in windows as a greeting to neighbours and a reminder of this special season. The little flickering flame looks very small against a dark window, but its light is cheering too. Sometimes the world seems a dark place. Lighting a Christmas candle can be a way of saying that we will not give up hope. There is an old proverb – *It is better to light one candle than to curse the darkness.*

> *It is God who has said, 'Let light shine out of darkness', who has shone in our hearts to give the light of the knowledge of the glory of God in the face of Christ.*
>
> 2 Corinthians 4:6

The sun sets on Edinburgh – from Calton Hill

# *Silent Night*

*Silent night, holy night.*
*All is calm, all is bright,*
*Round yon virgin mother and child;*
*Holy infant so tender and mild;*
*Sleep in heavenly peace,*
*Sleep in heavenly peace.*

*Joseph Mohr,*
*tr. J. Young*

One of the best loved carols, with a haunting tune, *Silent Night* was written as an emergency stop gap. A little European village church had problems with its organ. Mice had done such damage to the instrument that the special music planned for Christmas Day could not be used. A new carol was written in haste. No-one in the church could have guessed that it would be sung around the world with its message of reverence and peace.

The gaunt sandstone ruins of Whitby Abbey, Yorkshire

Outlined against the winter sky – the lovely spire of Norwich Cathedral

Christmas at Norwich Cathedral

# A Child is Born

*Joseph . . . went up from Galilee, from the city
of Nazareth, to Judea, to the city of David,
which is called Bethlehem, . . . to be enrolled
with Mary, his betrothed, who was with child.
And while they were there, the time came for her
to be delivered. And she gave birth to her first-
born son and wrapped him in swaddling cloths,
and laid him in a manger, because there was no
place for them in the inn.*

Luke 2:4-7

*For to us a child is born, to us a son is given; and
the government will be upon his shoulder, and
his name will be called 'Wonderful Counsellor,
Mighty God, Everlasting Father, Prince
of Peace'.*

Isaiah 9:6

ISBN 0-7117-0418-X © Copyright Jarrold Colour Publications 1989.
Designed and Produced by Parke Sutton Limited, Norwich for
Jarrold Colour Publications, Norwich.
Printed in Portugal.